Original title:
What's Life Without a Little Chaos?

Copyright © 2025 Creative Arts Management OÜ
All rights reserved.

Author: Vivian Laurent
ISBN HARDBACK: 978-1-80566-030-9
ISBN PAPERBACK: 978-1-80566-325-6

Whispers of Wild Currents

In the midst of jumbled socks,
A dancing dog in mismatched clogs.
Spinning plates on a wooden stake,
Life's circus, for goodness' sake!

A spilled drink leads to wild cheer,
As the cat zooms by, hold on, dear!
Confetti falls from the ceiling high,
Under this joyful, chaotic sky.

The Symphony of Unruly Moments

A trumpet blares from the kitchen pot,
And noodles launch from a boiling spot.
The toaster sings a tune so sweet,
While the fridge starts tapping its funny feet.

Juggling eggs with a smile so wide,
As the dog steals lunch with mischievous pride.
Life's a tune, a whimsical play,
Where rules are just tossed away.

Dance of the Disordered Heart

Waltzing with laundry on the floor,
Chasing after dreams at the front door.
A whirl of colors in a messy swirl,
Each tumble creates a chaotic twirl.

The clock ticks loud as dogs run by,
While socks unite in a pair goodbye.
With every bump, a laughter mixed,
Life's a riddle, delightfully fixed.

Embrace the Beautiful Mayhem

Paint splatters on the walls unite,
As kids break out in delight so bright.
A cupcake lands with a splat and cheer,
Creating chaos, yet we hold it dear.

Frogs in the bedroom, oh what a sight!
Each leap of fun a pure delight.
So let the laughter echo loud,
In our mess, let's be proud!

A Canvas of Colorful Uncertainty.

Splattered paint on canvas bright,
A turvy world, what a sight!
Paintbrush slipping, colors clash,
Oh, what a glorious splash!

Brush strokes dance, they trip and sway,
Creating laughter in a playful way.
A masterpiece within the mess,
Who needs deep calm? We love the excess!

Embrace the Beautiful Mess

Spilled coffee on the floor,
What a grand encore!
With sugar stuck to my shoe,
I'll say it's art, that much is true!

Every sock a different pair,
Laundry day? Who's aware!
Chaos reigns in laundry lands,
But I've got time for goofy plans!

Whispers in the Twisted Wind

Leaves swirling in a frolicsome twirl,
Catch the breeze, give it a whirl!
Kites tangled in the neighbor's tree,
Oh, the joy of wild jubilee!

Wind chimes clatter, birds take flight,
A mischievous dance, oh what delight!
Nature giggles in the gusty play,
As we embrace this zany ballet!

Symphony of Unraveled Threads

Knots in yarn like life's own song,
Pulling threads, can't go wrong!
Needles poking, fabric flies,
Sewing laughter under bright skies!

A stitch undone, a charming spree,
Tangled up, just let it be!
In each tangle, joy ascends,
Life's a quilt of joyful bends!

Tidal Waves of Unpredictability

Riding waves on a banana boat,
Screaming loud as I nearly float.
Crashing into sand, a laughing fit,
Who knew a day could be this lit?

A squirrel steals my fries with glee,
I chase it down, can't let it be.
With ketchup trails and hands all messy,
Life's little chaos makes me feel blessy.

Thriving in the Turbulent Dance

Twirl around in mismatched socks,
Dinner plans go out with clocks.
Stepping on my cat's long tail,
Now that's not part of my tale!

With coffee spills and laughter loud,
I embrace the chaos, feel so proud.
A dance-off breaks in the grocery line,
Where lemons roll, it's all just fine.

The Sweetness of Sweet Disarray

Pancakes flipped go soaring high,
Land on the dog, oh my, oh my!
Maple syrup drips like dreams,
Life's a giggle, bursting seams.

Untangled cords and missing shoes,
Throwing darts at morning news.
Who needs structure, anyway?
Let's embrace this messy play!

Finding Order in the Whirlwind

A sudden storm in my living room,
Tornado of cushions, could be my doom.
Yet I laugh as chaos reigns,
Sipping tea with wild refrains.

Lost my keys? Well, what a game!
Searching finds new things to claim.
In this swirl of "where'd it go?",
Disorder dances; it steals the show.

Finding Meaning in the Madness

In a world that's full of quirks,
A cat might dance in polka shirt.
The coffee spills upon the floor,
Yet somehow, we still crave for more.

A sock's lost battle in the wash,
It spins and twirls, a laundry posh.
Pet goldfish whispers secret plans,
While we pretend to understand.

Unruly Rhythms of the Universe

The stars have mischief in their glow,
While planets jig and lightly flow.
Cosmic beats make fish confuse,
As aliens eat space veggie stew.

Jellybeans may run the show,
While unicorns steal all the dough.
The sun forgot to rise today,
And night got lost in a cabaret.

Euphoria in the disarray

Pancakes fly like frisbees high,
While dogs debate the pie in the sky.
A rainbow's sneeze ignites the morn,
And cats compose a rock 'n roll horn.

Chickens jive in polka spots,
And alliterations tie their knots.
With chaos as the shining star,
Our whims are just as mad, bizarre.

Handwritten Chronicles of Life's Whirlwind

With crayons scribbled on a wall,
We write our tales through it all.
The toaster sings a morning tune,
As squirrels dance beneath the moon.

Life's too short for neat and prim,
So grab that chaos on a whim.
A hiccup leads to laughter's glow,
In every twist, the joy we'll sow.

Currents of Uncontainable Joy

In the blender of dreams, we laugh,
Spinning tales in the aftermath.
Dancing socks in mismatched pairs,
Life's a circus, no one cares.

Juggling troubles, what a show,
Falling pies and rubber toes.
We ride the waves, a bumpy boat,
Chasing chaos with a giddy float.

Silly hats on heads so grand,
Making memories, hand in hand.
With each tumble, a new surprise,
Laughter sparkles in our eyes.

So here we sway in pure delight,
Embracing mishaps, holding tight.
For in the mess, we find our peace,
A joyful chaos that won't cease.

Scattered Stars and Cosmic Whirls

Galaxies spin, the sky a mess,
Dancing comets wear a dress.
Stumbling dreams in cosmic play,
Chuckling stars, they giggle away.

Planets bump and wobble too,
A moonbeam slips, a cosmic boo!
Life's a ride on rainbow trails,
Sailing ships with floppy sails.

Raucous laughter fills the void,
Amidst the chaos, hearts are buoyed.
We twirl like sprites in neon light,
Finding joy in the wild flight.

And when the dust begins to clear,
We celebrate with an uproarious cheer.
For scattered stars and swirling dream,
Make life's tapestry brightly beam.

Portraits of the Serene and the Chaotic

In a world so neat and tidy,
A cat sat on my tea.
He knocked it off with glee,
And spilled my sanity.

A straight line is so boring,
Why not zigzag and twirl?
The fridge won't stop exploring,
As it turns into a whirl.

The socks play hide and seek,
Underneath my bed they creep.
In this peculiar leak,
Laundry seems to weep.

Yet in these little frays,
Laughter fills the air.
Embrace the wild displays,
A chaos without care.

Rhapsody of the Unhinged

Skipping steps, a waltz of clunk,
Like a hamster in a trunk.
Two left feet, who'd ever thunk?
The music's off, but who's the punk?

Coffee spills on my shirt,
A masterpiece of brown.
It's more than just a flirt,
It's a daily sort of crown.

Why bother finding calm?
When the chaos sings so loud.
It wraps you tight like balm,
In the madness, be proud.

So join the joyous mess,
Dance with socks, just don't trip.
Life's a crazy finesse—
Take a wildly great leap.

Chronicles of Beautiful Disruption

Once my plants went on a spree,
They threw a party for the bees.
With soil stains and sneezes,
They turned my house into their seas.

A blender broke in mid-air,
It launched strawberries around.
The walls now have flair,
Decorating with red "ground."

Mismatched spoons on the floor,
Forks rally for some fun.
The cupboard's now a lore,
Of kitchens on the run.

So when life's out of frame,
Celebrate the quirky play.
In chaos, we find fame,
In the wild, choose to stay.

Joy in the Jumble

One sock on the dog's head,
The other barks at the moon.
Who needs a straightened bed,
When the giggles start to croon?

Spilled paint on the floor,
A rainbow is now our guest.
No need to clean—ignore,
Art lives in this messy jest.

Eggs are set for disaster,
As they roll, they start to dance.
Who knew breakfast could master,
This whimsical, wild romance?

In the jumble we find cheer,
In chaos, life feels fair.
With laughter ringing clear,
Embrace the wild affair.

Kaleidoscope of Uncharted Paths

In a dance of colorful swirls,
Cats chase shadows, and laughter twirls.
Spilled milk makes artistic flair,
A bumpy ride, but who would care?

Jelly beans rained down from the sky,
Socks mismatch as they flutter by.
Life's a puzzle, pieces askew,
Yet here we are, just me and you.

An Ode to Unexpected Turns

A pizza's choice, pineapple thrill,
Dance like no one's home on the hill.
A squirrel steals fries, what a heist!
We toast to chaos, oh what a feast!

Rain falls sideways, umbrellas burst,
In every hiccup, there's joy, not thirst.
Shoes untied, they trip our plans,
But in that mess, laughter spans.

Tapestry Woven by Tempests

Spaghetti nights turned into wars,
Sauce on walls, with giggles galore.
Dishwashing's a splash contest, my friend,
When life throws lemons, let's just blend.

Tickles from feathers in a wild chase,
Puppies dive in, oh what a race!
A quilt of chaos, stitched with glee,
Who thought mayhem could feel so free?

Tracing Chaos with Poetic Fingers

Sketch a picture, but it's a doodle,
Plans gone rogue, life's little poodle.
A balloon floats off, waves goodbye,
Chasing dreams that zoom and fly.

Mismatched socks tell stories untold,
Every wrinkle is a journey bold.
With silly hats and ice cream stains,
We'll ride the whirlwinds, embrace the rains.

Capturing Whirlwinds in Verses

In the morning, socks don't match,
The coffee's cold, a tricky catch.
Chickens dance, the cat won't budge,
And here I am, a coffee judge.

Spilled cereal, a colorful mess,
While toddlers jump in a foam-filled dress.
The dog steals snacks with a sly little grin,
And life spins on, let the chaos begin!

Bikes upside down, the garden's a fright,
Who knew a flower could bloom overnight?
Neighbors peek through the curtains tight,
As laughter erupts at the silliest sight.

In whirls of chaos, we find surprise,
A spark of joy in the wildest skies.
With each twist, life's a merry dance,
Join in the fun, give chaos a chance!

Holiday in a Spiral

Pack your bags for a topsy trip,
Mismatched shorts with a ketchup drip.
The flight took off with a hiccup or two,
While a toddler's tantrum steals the view.

The beach ball bounces in unexpected ways,
It lands on a sunbather—what will she say?
Ice cream melts with a plop and a splatter,
While seagulls swoop down with a loud, mean chatter.

Flip-flops lost in the tide's wild race,
Finding them now feels like a chase.
A whirlwind of laughter, splashes and glee,
Join the havoc, come soak in the sea!

This holiday isn't your structured plan,
It's a wild ride, oh yes, if you can.
Dancing through chaos, we'll sing and shout,
With goofy grins, let the fun spin out!

Between the Lines of Pandemonium

A jelly jar flew, oh what a sight,
It glided through air, with sticky delight.
The dog chased its tail, a dizzy display,
While Uncle Joe just laughed all the way.

Birthday hats launched like rockets in flight,
Chasing down piñatas, oh what a fight!
Laughter erupts as balloons start to pop,
In this crazy circus, the fun will not stop.

The cake's on the floor, frosting everywhere,
While kids run like ninjas, no time for a care.
Between wild antics and playful fun,
We discover a world where life's never done.

So come join the dance, don't worry or fret,
In the rush of pandemonium, let's not forget.
We'll find joy in the mess, glee in the noise,
Life's better embraced with our silly joys!

Identifier of Disturbed Harmony

A sock monster lurks under the bed,
Devouring pairs, it's chaos well-fed.
The toaster spits crumbs, a breakfast war,
With burnt edges dancing, who could want more?

When the vacuum dances, it's a new kind of show,
And piles of laundry become a fort for slow.
Cats plotting wily schemes in the night,
While plants are deciding to take off in flight.

In this sweet mayhem, new friendships ignite,
As we share our mishaps with giggles so bright.
With chaos around us, let's stand up and cheer,
For the joy of the ride and the laughter we steer.

So raise a glass to the poorly timed joke,
As the chaos unfolds, let's lighten the yoke.
In life's raucous journey, let's cherish the sound,
Of laughter and mischief, where joy can be found!

The Dance of Tempestuous Dreams

In dreams, the ducks wear bow ties,
They tango beneath the stormy skies.
Cats on skateboards whiz on by,
While elephants attempt to fly.

A tree in a tutu twirls around,
As squirrels breakdance on the ground.
The clouds throw confetti in the air,
While chickens join without a care.

This party rages, wild and bright,
With disco balls in black and white.
The moon serves punch, a wobbly brew,
In this chaos, dreams come true.

Tomorrow's calm seems far away,
But who needs peace for a grand ballet?
Let's sway with the whirl, embrace the fun,
In the dance of the chaos, we're all one!

Wildflowers in a Raging Storm

Amidst the thunder, daisies sway,
They giggle at the sky's display.
Poppies wear shades, chilling out,
While tulips jump and twist about.

The rain makes water balloons galore,
Each droplet bursting, adding more.
Bees in boots do the cha-cha slide,
In this wild storm, there's nothing to hide.

A whirlwind of petals, oh what a sight,
As radishes dance in pure delight.
Ladybugs form a conga line,
While nature laughs, feeling divine.

So let the storm roll in with grace,
For every gust is a warm embrace.
Life without chaos is utterly tame,
Let's bloom and dance, it's all a game!

Songs from the Edge of Turmoil

From the depths of life's mad fray,
Comes a tune that's here to stay.
A chorus of cats sings loud and proud,
While gophers gather, forming a crowd.

The trumpets blast, made from old cans,
And turtles form a marching band.
Squirrels shout out, "What's the plan?"
As raccoons launch into a clapping jam.

In the chaos, the rhythm flows,
The music grows, and laughter glows.
A symphony born of wild surprise,
With chaos, life, it surely flies.

So let the songs emerge from strife,
In this turmoil, we find new life.
For every note finds a shining place,
In the wild embrace of chaotic grace.

Tornadoes of Emotion

In a whirlwind of feelings, we spin,
With laughter that echoes, where to begin?
A twirl of joy zips past the gloom,
While sadness plays a tambourine tune.

Frustration tosses its hair in the breeze,
As giggles flutter like little leaves.
Anger, with horns, shouts out in jest,
But beneath the chaos, we feel the best.

A hurricane of hugs swirls close by,
While thrills and spills make spirits fly.
In the tornado, we find our spark,
As laughter echoes from dawn till dark.

So hold on tight through the swirling ride,
Enjoy the chaos, let hearts collide.
For in this tempest, we learn to dance,
Embracing the wild, we find our chance.

Serendipity in the Storm

Raindrops tap dance on the roof,
Splashes in puddles bring joy, oh what goof.
Umbrella turned inside out, a sight to behold,
Laughter erupts, while the wind feels bold.

A cat in the rain, looks utterly shocked,
Chasing after shadows, while the clouds are locked.
Oh, what a symphony—nature's grand scheme,
In wild wet chaos, we laugh and we dream.

Chaos as Comedy in Everyday Life

The coffee spills just before the meet,
A misstep here, a slippery seat.
"Oh look at me," I laugh with flair,
As colleagues stare in disbelief, a dare.

The cat steals my lunch, a thief in the night,
Pasta flying; oh, what a sight!
In traffic jams, the horn's a new song,
Life's little mix-ups, where we all belong.

The Art of Embracing the Unexpected

A surprise party was planned for me,
Walked into chaos—who could it be?
Confetti in hair, balloons gone rogue,
I join the dance; revelry is the vogue.

Baking gone wrong, flour all over the floor,
Cookies that crumble and laugh till we roar.
Finding the joy in a burnt soufflé,
Oh, the art of chaos, come what may!

Fractured Patterns

Socks that never match, oh what a trend,
Stumbling through life, on laughter we depend.
Paint splatters like life's little blunders,
In the mess, we find joy, amidst all the wonders.

The scrunched-up paper tells tales untold,
Words gone awry, yet memories unfold.
A puzzle with pieces that never quite fit,
But in those odd shapes, we find the wit.

Perfect Chaos

Juggling tasks like a clown at the fair,
Life's little tussles, with flair we declare.
A spontaneous road trip, all turned about,
With snacks and silly songs, we laugh while we shout!

Dinner's a disaster, but spirits ignite,
Burnt toast and laughter are pure delight.
The magic's in mishaps; oh, can't you see?
In this perfect chaos, we're wild and free!

Fractured Glass

A cat walks by, slips on the floor,
The vase crashes down, oh, what a roar!
Shattered pieces scatter wide,
A mosaic of chaos, where secrets hide.

Mom's favorite cup, now just a joke,
Life throws curves, we merely poke.
Laughter erupts, no need to weep,
In broken shards, humor runs deep.

Priceless Reflections

Mirror, mirror, cracks in the sheen,
Who knew a sneeze could cause such a scene?
Each fracture a tale, a chuckle concealed,
In a funny way, the truth is revealed.

We dance through the chaos, we stumble and sway,
Every mishap a part of the play.
Priceless the laughter, worth more than gold,
In the absurd, our stories unfold.

Anarchy in the Garden of Dreams

In the garden, plants do misbehave,
Sunflowers dance while the daisies rave.
The gnome with the hat starts a raucous fight,
As ladybugs cheer, oh what a sight!

Worms join the fray, doing the twist,
The chaos of color intertwined with mist.
In this wild party, joy has its say,
We laugh at the mess; it's all part of play.

The Ballet of Broken Patterns

Twirling in circles, a soup of our plans,
Life's a ballet, led by clumsy hands.
We trip and we slide, all to the beat,
In the dance of the errant, we find our seat.

Foot in the cake, a stumble, a fall,
Laughter erupts, fills the hall.
A jester's delight, a comical chance,
In broken patterns, we learn how to dance.

Radiance in the Recklessness

Chaos blooms brightly, a vivid display,
Like a toddler with crayons, we color the day.
With giggles and shrieks, we let out a cheer,
In the messiness, we find what is dear.

Splatters of joy, paint on the walls,
We embrace the wildness, whatever befalls.
Life's radiant chaos, a beautiful spree,
In the reckless abandon, we're truly free.

Colors in a Stormy Palette

Raindrops splatter like paint on a wall,
Umbrellas flip, and some people fall.
A pigeon struts with its feathery flair,
While I sip coffee, without a care.

Laughter erupts as the thunder claps,
Cats run frantic, the dog takes laps.
Colors bleed from the overcast skies,
Life's jigsaw puzzle has no goodbyes.

People in puddles make quite the scene,
And I find myself lost in the routine.
Gumboots clash with the wildest socks,
Stepping over stains and quirky blocks.

Chaos paints laughter with each stormy gust,
We're all just a brush on the canvas of dust.
Let's dance with the lightning, twirl with the rain,
Embrace the shimmer, forget all the pain.

Tides of Unpredictable Harmony

Waves crash loudly, a surfer's delight,
Fins and flip-flops take flight every night.
The moon pulls strings on a tangled beach,
As sandcastles sway, just out of reach.

Children squeal at the jellyfish glow,
While ice cream melts in a colorful flow.
Seagulls complain as they steal my fries,
And I'm left chuckling, watching their lies.

Each tide hands chaos a rhythm and beat,
As flip-flops get lost in the shuffle of feet.
The shoreline dances in laughter and glee,
A symphony crafted by nature's decree.

Life's a jumble of jokes and surprises,
With playful dolphins and friendly disguises.
So surf on the waves of the wacky and wild,
We're all just the ocean's exuberant child.

Dance on the Edge of Chaos

Balancing acts on a tightrope of fun,
But who needs a plan when you can just run?
Twirling and swirling, the clowns make their mark,
With pies flying high, and laughter's the spark.

The jester tips over, it's all gone awry,
While onlookers giggle, oh me, oh my!
Confetti the color of squishy marshmallows,
Floats through the air like magical bellow.

Giggles and wiggles from everyone near,
As chaos dances, we cheer and we cheer.
A juggle of moments, a tumble, a fall,
And then a grand leap with a flourish for all.

Spin with the mayhem on shoes too big,
You'll find joy in the chaos, a cake that's a jig.
Life is a circus, no need for a cue,
Embrace every tumble; they're just part of the view!

Serenade of the Misfit Heart

A heart that beats out of rhythm and rhyme,
Counts to the clatter, a dance out of time.
Like a cat who sings in the dead of the night,
Its melody clashes with moonbeams so bright.

Socks lost in laundry take center stage,
As mismatched shoes dance, unlocking the cage.
With every stumble, a laugh and a twirl,
The offbeat serenade begins to unfurl.

The world spins gleefully, wobbles and shakes,
A burrito on wheels makes hilarious breaks.
Life's an adventure, a jigsaw unsolved,
The more that it tumbles, the more we evolve.

Raise a glass to the weird and the wild,
Celebrate every misstep, each heart like a child.
In the symphony of chaos, no notes go unheard,
Join the raucous chorus, let laughter be stirred!

The Technicolor of Turbulence

Colors burst and blend anew,
The cat's on the table, what shall we do?
Spilled paint and laughter fill the air,
Life's vibrant chaos is everywhere.

Juggling dreams in the carnival glow,
One step forward, two to and fro.
Cupcakes fly as we dance and twirl,
In this circus, we're all a whirl!

Tangled strings of a kite in flight,
Who knew chaos could feel so right?
The echoes of joy, across the sky,
In the mess, our giggles can fly.

With every turn, we take a chance,
A wobbly ride, come join the dance!
Funnel cake and wild confetti,
In this tempest, we grow unsteady.

Fragments of a Flawed Serenity

A quiet day turns wild and free,
The laundry attacks, oh dear me!
Socks in the toaster, how can this be?
Serenity's shattered, just wait and see.

The dog chases shadows, let's not resist,
He leaps on the couch, a jump with a twist.
Pillows in chaos, feathers in flight,
This tranquil scene has taken a bite.

Tea spills on the carpet, much to my fright,
The cat's in the fray, ready to fight.
But giggles erupt, as we sigh and swap,
Finding pure bliss in this topsy-trop.

So we raise our cups, and toast to the fun,
In life's lovely madness, we all become one.
Fragments of peace in delightful disarray,
Here's to the chaos that leads us astray!

The Mischief of Life's Twists

With a leap and a bound, we're off on a ride,
Dancing on edges where chaos can hide.
A pie in the face is our laughter's decree,
In this wacky journey, just come follow me!

The road's uneven, but we won't complain,
Every turn promises a new type of gain.
Silly mishaps, like balding a cat,
Life throws its curveballs, how 'bout that?

Chasing bright rainbows that lead us astray,
With jellybeans falling on a Wednesday play.
Supportive pals in their mismatched socks,
Fizzing with fun, we're unorthodox!

In every twist, there's a chuckle to find,
Joining the mayhem, I gladly unwind.
With a wink and a nod, we embrace the odd,
Living our lives like it's grounded in fog!

Mirth in the Madness

A hopscotch of blunders, oh what a sight,
Life's little puzzles bring sheer delight.
With mismatched shoes and hair askew,
In the madness, happiness breaks through!

A splash of mischief makes hearts take flight,
When the dog steals lunch in the broad daylight.
Pranks on the friends keep the smiles alive,
Together we twist, revel and strive.

The cake has collapsed, but spirits won't droop,
We'll gather the crumbs and form a new group.
With giggles like bubbles that float in the breeze,
We'll savor the chaos just like a tease.

So here's to the fun in each quirky pitfall,
To the slip-ups that catch us, and the rise after all.
In this vibrant dance of unpredictable glee,
Mirth in the madness is where we're meant to be!

Dancing Through the Disarray

In my kitchen, pots collide,
Spaghetti's dancing, can't hide!
The cat is leaping, what a sight,
While I'm tangled in sheer delight.

Coffee spills like crazy rain,
I laugh, ignore the growing stain.
My socks are mismatched, what a trend,
Fashion's chaos, I can't pretend!

Chairs are stacked like towers high,
Underneath, a lost shoe sighs.
We twirl through mess, embrace the norm,
In this wild, chaotic swarm!

Life's a dance, so twist and spin,
Who needs routine when you win?
With every slip, a giggle loud,
In this muddled joy, we are proud!

The Art of Delightful Disorder

Paint splatters on my walls anew,
A masterpiece, just ask my crew!
Brushes scattered, oh what fun,
Imperfect strokes by everyone.

Dishes piled like a jigsaw game,
Who will win? It's all the same.
The cupboard's bare but spirits high,
Chasing snacks while we all sigh.

Neighbors wonder what's the fuss,
As laughter echoes 'round the bus.
We write our tales of chaotic grace,
With every hiccup, a smiling face!

Worn-out shoes and hair askew,
A wild life is our debut!
So toast to mess and cheers to fun,
In this bright disorder, we've won!

Poems from an Unkempt Heart

My heart's a cluttered, wild affair,
With socks and dreams flung everywhere!
Each messy thought, a treasure chest,
Where chaos sings and jokes won't rest.

Dinner plans made on a whim,
Burnt toast dancing at the rim.
Laughter's flavor, a quirky spice,
In our delightful slice of life.

Stumbling through the laundry heap,
Lost in giggles, my heart will leap.
The world's a stage, we twist and twirl,
In the beauty of this messy whirl!

So let's embrace the tangled bits,
With silly quirks, our spirit fits!
In unkempt bliss, we find our sound,
Each joyful uproar, love unbound.

Chaotic Melodies of Existence

Life's a concert, loud and bright,
With off-key notes that feel just right.
Every missed beat, a silly charm,
In disarray, we find our calm.

We juggle errands, shop and dash,
A puzzle made of crazy flash.
Grocery lists in total dismay,
Yet laughter leads us on our way.

Silly songs in mismatched shoes,
Dropping beats like nothing's new.
Let's waltz through chaos, twirl with glee,
In this funny dance, just you and me!

The world's our stage, our hearts are free,
In every blunder, pure harmony.
With chaotic tunes, we'll sing and play,
In this ensemble, we'll find our way!

The Charm of Beautiful Imperfection

Wobbly cakes and crooked lines,
A dance of flaws, where joy entwines.
We trip and laugh, we scrape our knees,
In the art of life, we aim to please.

Mismatched socks and tangled hair,
A symphony of chaos in the air.
Through every blunder, we find our way,
In the beautiful messiness of each day.

Spilled coffee on the crossword clue,
A puzzle now, but that's okay too.
With every error, a chuckle grows,
In perfect imperfection, our spirit glows.

So raise your glass to every slip,
In this grand circus, let's take our trip.
For life's a canvas of vibrant hues,
With every flaw, there's more to muse.

Serenade to the Shattered Norm

On a Tuesday, I wore my shirt inside out,
The look on their faces, a curious shout.
Why follow rules that make us so bland?
In this goofy orchestra, let's form a band.

Math says four, but I count to five,
With every hiccup, I feel alive.
Messy desks and derailed routines,
In the symphony of life, we're the unseen queens.

Jumping puddles in shoes not meant,
Who cares if my time and plan are spent?
In broken schedules and lost to-dos,
We find a freedom that's ours to choose.

So here's a tune to the wreckage we find,
In each shattered norm, a vibrant grind.
Let's twirl in the chaos, dance with a smile,
For laughter's the melody that lasts a while.

The Poetry of Punctured Plans

I mapped my day, each hour a gem,
But life had other thoughts for them.
The coffee spill, the socks that fade,
Oh, how those grand designs have strayed!

A meeting missed, a flat tire song,
Yet somehow, I feel I still belong.
In fate's wild games, I find delight,
As plans unfold in twists so bright.

The recipe flops, the cake won't rise,
Yet laughter fills my kitchen—oh, the surprise!
With every mishap, stories grow,
In the rhythm of chaos, we steal the show.

So here's to the days with errant turns,
In unexpected paths, curiosity burns.
For with every puncture, there's a chance,
To explore and laugh in life's wild dance.

Where Clarity Meets Confusion

On Mondays, I search for my car keys,
While the cat's plotting a world tour, if you please.
With tangled thoughts and jumbled plans,
Life giggles softly, ignoring my scans.

The GPS blinks, then goes on strike,
To find my way, I'll just hike.
In the blend of lost and found,
The joy of confusion spins all around.

Every question marks a new delight,
In laughter's echo, we take flight.
With each misstep, a truth aligns,
Where clarity winks and chaos shines.

So cheers to the puzzles that leave us bemused,
In this playful chaos, we're happily bruised.
For life's finest tales are often unclear,
Yet spark joy and laughter each time they appear.

The Joyful Fracture

In a world of wedged-up shoes,
Laughter dances through the blues.
Socks mismatched, it's quite a sight,
Who needs order when there's delight?

Splattered paint, a canvas mess,
An artful chaos, we confess.
Brushes clashing, colors scream,
Life's a vibrant, wobbly dream.

Dinner's burnt, the cat's on fire,
A symphony of chaos, we require.
Spaghetti twirls in wild romance,
In the madness, we find our dance.

So toast the spills and blunders bold,
With every mishap, stories unfold.
A joyful fracture, not a frown,
In the chaos, we wear the crown.

Chaos, the Muse of Creation

Juggling eggs with glee and grace,
Eggshells scatter, what a race!
Creativity's wild, a spinning spree,
Messy hands, it's pure jubilee.

In a whirlwind of papers and dreams,
Ideas collide in quirky themes.
From chaos springs the brightest spark,
Inventive minds create their mark.

Loud laughter echoes, crumbs in the air,
As we embark on joyous dare.
Crafting wonder from a tangled web,
Life's a giggle, pull the ebb.

So let the mayhem lead the way,
In every slip, we find our play.
Chaos whispers, "Join the fun!"
In this dance, we all are one.

The Enigma of Entangled Hearts

Two left feet on a crowded floor,
We trip and tumble, laugh some more.
In tangled hearts, chaos reigns,
Love's a mix of joys and pains.

His socks, my dress; a blend of hues,
In a circus, we can't refuse.
With every quirk and silly twist,
We find the magic in the mist.

Bumps and bruises, we wear with pride,
In chaos' arms, we often bide.
What's life without a glorious fuss?
We embrace the chaos, just because.

Entangled hearts, dancing brave,
In our jumbled love, we misbehave.
A riddle wrapped in laughter's glow,
In the mess, our true love shows.

Comets of Chaos and Wonder

In the sky, we see them fly,
Comets blazing, oh my, oh my!
Streaks of light through midnight's haze,
Chasing dreams in wild arrays.

Kitchen experiments gone awry,
Splatters dropping, oh my oh my!
Clever concoctions, who knew it could?
In every blunder, the world feels good.

Cards on tables flipping fast,
As laughter echoes, we hold on fast.
Games of chance lead to sheer delight,
In the chaos, we ignite the night.

So here's to comets, bold and bright,
Spinning through chaos, a wondrous sight.
In flicks of mishap, joy unfurled,
What fun awaits in our crazy world!

Lively Tumults of the Soul

In a world of topsy-turvy, things go amiss,
Coffee spills on papers, can't find my kiss.
Birds sing out of tune, dogs chase their tails,
We dance through the mess, ignoring the gales.

Frogs in a tuxedo jump over the moon,
Cats are the conductors, they'll sing us a tune.
Each step's a little wobbly, laughter ensues,
Chaos brings us joy in the wildest of hues.

Late-night snacks are barter for dreams gone astray,
With socks that don't match, we just laugh and play.
Here's to the fluster, the twirls and the spins,
Life's a grand carnival, let the chaos begin!

In juggling our troubles, we find silly grace,
Lost in a whirlwind, it's a merry race.
With each puzzled glance and every blunder spree,
We cherish the chaos, come laugh with me!

A Canvas of Spiraling Moments

Life's like a painting, with colors that clash,
A splash of confusion, a bright, silly flash.
Brush strokes of chaos, swirl in delight,
We giggle at mishaps that brighten the night.

Potatoes in spacesuits and cats in the fray,
Dance on the tables, they twirl and display.
A bubblegum symphony plays all around,
In the mess we've created, pure joy can be found.

With whirlwinds of laughter, and flips of the plot,
As socks start to vanish, we care not a jot.
Life's wild, unruly, it's something to cheer,
Each twist is a treasure, it's chaos we revere!

So let's paint the ceilings, let chaos adorn,
With smiles that are crooked and feelings reborn.
In this masterpiece spun, where giggles reside,
Let chaos be the muse, our quirky guide!

Embracing Elysium's Entropy

In a land of delightful disarray,
Shenanigans dance, leading hearts in play.
Checkered paths of laughter, where reason falls flat,
We wander through whimsy, tipping our hat.

Juggling all sorts, from pickles to pies,
We cheer for the mess, where chaos complies.
Silly stunts abound as we twirl through the air,
Life's wobbly hammock, we tumble without care.

Tangled in colors, like spaghetti on walls,
We stumble through chaos, hear laughter's calls.
In this tangled tapestry, joy outshines dread,
With each silly mishap, new memories spread.

So raise up a toast, to the wacky, the wild,
Embrace every moment—the dream of a child.
With laughter as our anthem, chaos our dance,
We sway to the rhythm of fate's wild romance!

Navigating the Beautiful Mayhem

Life's like a circus, with clowns on the floor,
Juggling our worries, we laugh evermore.
With pies in the face and balloons in the air,
We twirl through the chaos, without a care.

Wobbly bicycles race down the street,
Socks on our hands, oh, what a treat!
A horse in a tutu now prances about,
In this vibrant mayhem, we dance and we shout.

With ping pong balls rolling, and giggles that ring,
Life's a messy canvas that chaos can bring.
In the whirl of the absurd, we find our delight,
With each kooky moment, the world feels just right.

So let's not be cautious, embrace the wild way,
For amidst the confusion, joy tends to stay.
In this beautiful mayhem, cheers fill the air,
With a wink and a smile, we thrive without care!

Echoes of Harmonious Chaos

In the dance of socks, mismatched and free,
Laundry piles up like a wild jubilee.
Cats take the stage, on the curtains they swing,
Life's little messes are the best kind of fling.

Dinner's an enigma, spices thrown wide,
With a pinch of confusion, oh what a ride!
Flavors collide like a humorous band,
In the chaos of cooking, no plan goes as planned.

Kids in a whirl, like leaves in the breeze,
Painting the walls with wild, messy cheese.
Giggles erupt, while the dog wags his tail,
In the midst of the ruckus, they triumph, they sail.

So here's to the disarray, cheers loud and proud,
In the tapestry of chaos, we're comfortably vowed.
With laughter as glue, and madness the thread,
In this kooky adventure, we're joyfully led.

Revelry in Disarray

A cake on the floor, oh what a scene,
Frosting on faces, all covered in green.
Balloons fly away, what a comical sight,
In the revelry of chaos, we dance in delight.

Tangled fairy lights, like snakes in a tangle,
We weave through the mess, and do a cool jangle.
Who needs perfection in a merry parade?
With chaos as music, let our hearts be laid.

The pets join the fun, a parade of their own,
While we trip on the toys that are widely strewn.
Laughter erupts as we tumble and soar,
In the heart of the chaos, we always want more.

So raise a toast high to our whimsical state,
Embrace all the jumbles, let happiness rate.
In each twist and turn, in every wild play,
We celebrate life in a charming dismay.

The Magic in Life's Unscripted Drama

A spelling bee morphs into a dance-off spree,
With every wrong word, we laugh with such glee.
A plot twist emerges, no script to confide,
In this unscripted drama, we take it in stride.

Unexpected visitors dressed as the night,
They bumble and tumble, what a wild sight!
Baking cookies leads to a flour-filled fight,
In the mess of our moments, everything's bright.

A kitchen revolution, we're chefs on the run,
With salt falling down like sparkles of fun.
In chaotic moments, the best tales arise,
Laughter and chaos are our sweetest surprise.

So here's to the blunders, let's raise a cheer,
In this grand adventure, we hold chaos dear.
For magic unfolds when we let down our guard,
In the theater of life, the antics are starred.

The Unexpected Grace of Turmoil

A spilled drink becomes a splash zone for all,
Twirling in chaos, we're having a ball.
With laughter abound and joy on display,
There's magic in turmoil that lights up our way.

A puzzle half-finished, pieces everywhere,
We laugh at the mess, as we dance in midair.
Life takes a turn, like a wobbly ride,
In the back of the bus, there's no need to hide.

With shoes on the table and phones on the floor,
His poker face cracks, oh what a funny score!
Let's throw out the plans, let spontaneity reign,
In the flavors of chaos, we dance in the rain.

So here's to the bumps, the quirks, and the fun,
In the grace of disarray, we've truly begun.
With hearts full of laughter, we'll never outgrow,
The unexpected wonders that chaos can show.

Fragile Harmony Amidst the Turbulence

In a world of wobbling plates,
Dancing spoons and wild mates,
Cats in hats play cards with glee,
While dogs chase their tails, oh me!

Juggling dreams with hands so small,
Avoiding chaos, always a brawl,
Yet laughter bubbles like a brook,
In the mayhem, take a look!

Chairs are spinning, socks astray,
Tissues flutter, come what may,
A serenade of kitchen fights,
As chaos holds us through the nights.

But in the noise, joy finds a way,
As clowns and confetti steal the day,
Life's a circus, wild and free,
We ride the waves, just you and me!

Hummingbirds in a Vortex

Buzzing birds in dizzy flight,
Spinning round like blurs of light,
A whirlwind of flaps and flicks,
Nature's zany bag of tricks.

Sippers clash at nectar streams,
Humming tunes in chaotic dreams,
Frenzied wings, a colorful parade,
In this chaos, joy is made.

Round and round, the whirlwinds twirl,
As tiny bodies dance and swirl,
With each sip, they chase delight,
In this whirlwind, a comical sight.

Though the world spins fast and loud,
These little sprites are never cowed,
For in their laughter, life explodes,
In this chaos, happiness unfolds!

Nature's Wildest Brush Strokes

Trees wearing hats of swirling leaves,
Rivers giggling, playful thieves,
Mountains wobble like old friends,
In nature's art, the fun never ends.

Colors clash in wild display,
Rabbits breakdance, hip-hip-hooray,
While clouds toss popcorn up high,
Nature's comedy slides by.

The wind whispers jokes in the breeze,
Tickling flowers, bringing them to tease,
Bees buzz in harmony, a chorus so sweet,
While ants form a line, a silly retreat.

In the mix of hues, laughter blooms,
Chaos of colors, wild costumes,
Life paints with brushes, flinging glee,
In this masterpiece, come dance with me!

Crescendo of Tumultuous Hearts

Hearts beat like drums in the fray,
While lovebirds squawk, come what may,
Harmonies clash in the moonlit night,
As hearts twirl in a comical flight.

Muffled giggles hide behind walls,
Spinning dreams in chaotic balls,
Plateaus of laughter drop and soar,
As we tumble through life's open door.

Twists and turns, the heart takes lead,
A symphony of hearts in wild need,
With joyful chaos in every beat,
Our lives syncopate to laughter's heat.

So let the tempests howl and roar,
For in this mess, we find our score,
With love as the melody, quick and spry,
In chaos, let our spirits fly!

The Chaos Within the Calm

In the quiet of the room, a sock takes flight,
Chasing dust bunnies in a wild delight.
Tea spills and dinners burn, oh what a sight,
Yet laughter erupts, turning wrongs to right.

Cats orchestrate the living room race,
As the dog joins in with sheer, goofy grace.
Melodies of clatter make a joyful space,
Who knew chaos could have such a face?

The clock ticks backward, what a strange trend,
Keys vanish like magic, where'd they descend?
But in this merry mess, friendships extend,
In a muddled world, there's fun to lend.

So let your heart dance in this playful storm,
Embrace the sweet madness, lovely as a warm,
For in this wild whirl, we all transform,
Finding joy in havoc is the true norm.

Helix of Madness and Joy

Spaghetti uncooked, it flies through the air,
An angelic noodle with wonders to share.
Pasta! It curls, with sauces to dare,
In this twirling dance, we find our flair.

The calendar shouts, 'Time's slipping away!'
But we laugh at timelines, come what may.
Juggling our whims in a curious play,
In this sweet chaos, we savor our day.

Bubbles and giggles are flying about,
As the world around spins in joyful shout.
Embracing the quirks, no need for a pout,
In our helix of madness, love's what it's about.

So why chase perfection, or order and peace?
In freestyle fun, let the craziness cease.
With laughter and smiles, our hearts find release,
In this joyful chaos, we find our increase.

Flight Patterns of the Unpredictable

Birds in a flurry, taking wild dives,
Chasing the wind with their quirky lives.
A squirrel auditions for lofty high fives,
In this madcap world, enthusiasm thrives.

Umbrellas flip, singing songs in the rain,
A dance of misfits twirling free from the mundane.
Lost in the shuffle, we play this game,
In the unpredictability, we claim our fame.

Coffee cups tipped in a vibrant parade,
As laughter bubbles, our worries cascade.
Here, the mundane gets joyously laid,
In this flight of fancy, traditions are frayed.

So toss all your plans to the skies above,
Let spontaneity lift you like a dove.
In the pattern of chaos, we find what we love,
As unpredictable wonders gently shove.

Freefalling in Beautiful Disorder

In the middle of a tumble, we lose our grace,
Yet every misstep holds magic to embrace.
With splattered paint and a splashed cupcake face,
In this beautiful ride, we find our place.

Books stacked high, a tower that sways,
Some call it a mess, but we call it a phase.
With giggles and chaos, we savor our days,
In the whirlwind of life, joy invariably plays.

Surprises like confetti rain from the sky,
With each scoop of chaos, we reach for the pie.
Twirling through mayhem, we'll just give it a try,
In this freefalling dance, we learn how to fly.

So let's leap into laughter, abandon all fear,
For life's sweetest moments are drawn ever near.
In disorder's embrace, friendships play clear,
As we freefall together, the fun reappears.

Wild Hearts and Whimsical Roads

In a world where socks do flee,
The cat plots mischief, oh so free.
We dance on clouds, absurd and bright,
Chasing shadows into the night.

The coffee spills, a morn's delight,
While birds take flight in sheer delight.
With every twist, a laugh erupts,
Life's bumpy ride just interrupts.

A goat in a hat? Oh, what a sight!
We'll paint our dreams in hues of white.
And on this road, let's make our stand,
Embrace the wild, the unplanned grand!

So let's stomp puddles, let joy unfold,
In this circus of chaos, hearts bold.
For in the mess, is where we find,
The laughter, the love, and the wild unwind!

Exploring the Unfurling Madness

A rubber duck floats in the stew,
While dancing llamas steal the view.
The doors of reason creak and groan,
As we chuckle at the unknown.

In pajamas worn to the store,
We juggle dreams, and maybe more.
The candy rain makes us all giddy,
Oh, the joy in the non-serious city!

The spoon says, 'Let's race a cup!'
While mischief waits to fill us up.
With each odd turn, we'll conquer fear,
And toast to chaos with a cheer!

So let's embark on this wild quest,
Where everyday nonsense feels the best.
With laughter loud, let's flip the story,
In a world where chaos is all our glory!

A Fractal Memory of Everyday Life

Fractals dance in our morning toast,
A whispering cat, our daily ghost.
The socks in pairs just can't be found,
In this waltz of life where weirdness abounds.

We ride our bikes upside down,
Chasing squirrels through the town.
With every giggle, a twist appears,
Our chaotic dance ignites the cheers.

From spilled drinks to charming mishaps,
Life's little quirks are gentle taps.
We're painting outside of the lines,
Woven threads of laughter are our signs.

So join the fun, let's sing out loud,
With tangled thoughts, we're chaos proud.
In this beautiful mess, joy's our strife,
A fractal memory of everyday life!

Echoes of the Unsung Disorder

Whispers of chaos in the hall,
The poster says, 'Let's have a ball!'
A dance-off in mismatched shoes,
Joyful mishaps, always good news.

Sorrows blocked by a rampaging cat,
While we ponder why birds wear hats.
Quirky tunes on repeat, so sweet,
In gentle pandemonium, we meet.

With tickles and giggles, the day unfolds,
In the pockets of chaos, life multiplies and molds.
Embrace the noise, let laughter roar,
In the symphony of madness, there's always more!

So when the world spins, let's find our way,
In the echoing laughter, let's play today.
For in this unsung disorder we thrive,
Celebrating the chaos that makes us alive!

Defying Order: The Poetry of Chaos

When socks get lost in the dryer space,
It's a sock sock revolution, what a wild place!
Dinner's on fire, and the cat's in a trance,
Chaos invites us, let's join in the dance.

The calendar's jumbled, what's today? Who cares?
Spontaneous road trips, life flares up in pairs.
From spilled coffee mornings to woozy-eyed nights,
Embrace the disorder, it fuels our delights.

Puppies run rampant, the curtains take flight,
Who knew that chasing would stir such delight?
With laughter we tumble, we wiggle and squirm,
In the grand scheme of things, it's us who affirm.

So here's to the chaos, our whimsical stew,
In a world full of order, we're breaking right through!
We'll twirl through the madness, not miss a beat,
For in lovely disarray, our hearts skip a beat.

Bonfire of the Unruly Spirits

Gather the misfits, let's light up the night,
Marshmallows and giggles, the mood's just right.
Unruly spirits, let's dance in the flames,
With every wild laugh, we're changing the games.

A broom on the ceiling, our thoughts in a swirl,
The cat's got a feather, oh see how they twirl!
In tinfoil hats, we'll declare our own fun,
Underneath all the stars, we're the favored ones.

With stories ignited, our hearts all aglow,
We're reveling wildly in the chaos we know.
Laughter erupts like a chorus so free,
In this bonfire of life, it's the best place to be.

So join in the madness, throw caution away,
In the warmth of our laughter, let's all dance and sway!
We'll roast every worry, and eat them with glee,
As the flames flicker brightly, it's pure jubilee.

Laughter Amidst Hurricane Winds

The winds howled loudly, a merriment's roar,
As we built our sandcastles, then lost them to shore.
With umbrellas turned inside out like a kite,
Laughter erupts as we dance with delight.

We circled through puddles and jumped like the frogs,
Singing our songs with the dogs and the logs.
On a carnival ride, upside down with a smile,
In the heart of the storm, let's stay for a while.

Chaos a-brewing? Oh, let the fun reign,
With soda explosions, we'll dance in the rain.
Life's little squabbles are humor in the mix,
In the hurricane's sway, we find all our tricks.

So let's raise our hats to this thrilling spree,
For laughter blooms wildly, on winds wild and free.
We ride every wave, we'll spin 'round and grin,
In the tumultuous dance, let the party begin!

The Grace in Brokenness

When the vase took a tumble, oh what a sight,
Shards on the floor, but it feels just right.
In every mishap, there's laughter to share,
Grace found in chaos, we handle with flair.

A pizza delivery? The door's not in the same,
A riddle or puzzle, it's part of the game.
Spaghetti explosion, sauce on the wall,
We're dining like kings in our grand buffet hall.

The universe chuckles, sends quirks our way,
With each little blunder, we live out our play.
In brokenness blooming, we flourish and roam,
Dancing with joy, we create our own home.

So embrace every fumble, each trip and each fall,
In the quilt made of chaos, we find the most haul.
Together we weave all our laughter and grace,
In the messy entanglements, we find our own place.

www.ingramcontent.com/pod-product-compliance
Lightning Source LLC
Chambersburg PA
CBHW071846160426
43209CB00003B/441